May God Bless you
through another day

Pepa

Soul Retreats

Rémy

Presented To

Papa

Presented By

12/25/05

Date

Soul Retreats™ *for Students*
ISBN 0-310-80187-7

Copyright 2003 by GRQ Ink, Inc.
Franklin, Tennessee 37067
"Soul Retreats" is a trademark owned by GRQ, Inc.

Published by Inspirio™, The gift group of Zondervan
5300 Patterson Avenue, SE
Grand Rapids, Michigan 49530

Requests for information should be addressed to:
Inspirio™, The gift group of Zondervan
Grand Rapids, Michigan 49530

http://www.inspiriogifts.com

Editor and Compiler: Lila Empson
Associate Editor: Janice Jacobson
Project Manager: Tom Dean
Manuscript written by Kevin D. Miller in conjunction with Snapdragon Editorial Group, Inc.
Design: Whisner Design Group

03 04 05/HK/ 4 3 2 1

Soul Retreats
for Students

inspirio™

Contents

Introduction

Time for yourself. Time to think, time to grow, time to find out what lies inside you. Experts say that's what everyone needs. But where do you find that time with classes, exams, and papers to write?

Soul Retreats™ for Students is designed to provide a variety of retreats—pick-me-ups for your soul as you go about the business of getting an education. These thirty retreats will show you how to capture a little time for yourself by opening your eyes to simple ways to replenish your inner resources through such activities as music, humor, friendship, and exercise.

Browse through the retreat titles and choose a selection each day that interests you, or simply read the retreats in the order they appear. Either way, you will discover encouragement, strength, and insight directed specifically to you as a student.

Their Casual Air

He sat inside a coffee shop
And sipped a Latin brew.
She relaxed upon the grass outside
And read a tale or two.
While I rushed about
For I know not what
And envied their casual air.

Ed Strauss

The Joy of Illumination

A Moment to Pause

If you find yourself struggling to keep your enthusiasm for school alive, step away for a moment and find a quiet place. It might be the backseat of the bus, a shady place below the bleachers, an empty classroom—anywhere you are comfortable and can find privacy. Now sit back and rest your eyes.

It must seem at times like you can't stuff one more bit of information into your head. And tomorrow is likely to be the same. Lessons, lessons, and more lessons. It's easy to lose the joy of learning amidst the crush of facts and figures.

If you think you can't put one more piece of information into your already overcrowded brain, try this: Settle on one thing, one bright and beautiful concept, one glowing, newly discovered fact, one small but powerful piece of information. This can be anything you choose—a new word, a profound thought, a never-before-considered idea, a far-out concept. Nurture this small treasure in your mind, allowing God to illuminate and expand it.

Expect God to take this one concept and inspire you with new ideas. Let these ideas move in and around and through your mind, easing the pressing obligation to learn and renewing your sense of excitement and anticipation.

Though it cost all you have, get understanding.
Esteem wisdom, and she will exalt you; embrace
her, and she will honor you.
—PROVERBS 4:7–8 NIV

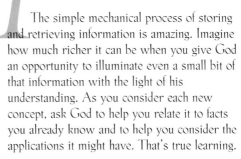

A Moment to Reflect

The simple mechanical process of storing and retrieving information is amazing. Imagine how much richer it can be when you give God an opportunity to illuminate even a small bit of that information with the light of his understanding. As you consider each new concept, ask God to help you relate it to facts you already know and to help you consider the applications it might have. That's true learning.

Find a few minutes whenever possible to retreat to a place where your mind and soul can be refreshed and renewed by God. Expect to come away with an education that will provide you with enthusiasm and inspiration throughout your life.

As thought by thought is piled,
Till some great truth
Is loosened,
And the nations
Echo round,
Shaken to their roots,
As do the mountains now.

—Percy Bysshe Shelley

9

*For the one who pleases him God gives wisdom
and knowledge and joy.*
Ecclesiastes 2:26 NRSV

A Moment to Refresh

*Do not be conformed to this world, but be
transformed by the renewing of your minds, so
that you may discern what is the will of God.*
Romans 12:2 NRSV

*Whatever is true, whatever is noble, whatever
is right, whatever is pure, whatever is
admirable—if anything is excellent or
praiseworthy—think about such things.*
Philippians 4:8 NIV

*The LORD gives wisdom; from his mouth come
knowledge and understanding.*
Proverbs 2:6 NRSV

Let the wise listen and add to their learning.
Proverbs 1:5 NIV

One thought driven home is better than three left on base.

—JAMES LITER

Within your temple, O God, we meditate on your unfailing love.

Psalm 48:9 NIV

To set the mind on the Spirit is life and peace.

Romans 8:6 NRSV

I have more insight than all my teachers, for I meditate on your statutes.

Psalm 119:99 NIV

Set your hearts on things above, where Christ is seated at the right hand of God. Set your minds on things above, not on earthly things.

Colossians 3:1–2 NIV

The mind is like the stomach. It is not how much you put into it that counts, but how much it digests.

—ALBERT JAY NOCK

Keeping the Dream Alive

A Moment to Pause

Step back—even if it's just for a few minutes—and ask God to renew your vision. This is particularly helpful to do when you find yourself so focused on the process and problems of getting an education that you lose sight of your reason, your dream, and your inner vision for what you want to do with your life. It's easy to understand how that could happen with exams and class schedules screaming for your attention.

Find a comfortable place to stretch out. Then consciously release any thoughts of paper deadlines and upcoming exams. Ask God to stir up within you the inner dream of what it will be like when you have achieved your educational goals. Ask him to help you see yourself doing that one thing your education is preparing you to do.

If you plan to be a doctor, see yourself caring for a patient. If you want to be a teacher, see yourself interacting with your students. If you dream of being a writer, see yourself writing your first book. If you desire to be an entrepreneur, see yourself putting action to your vision. Give God an opportunity to seal your dreams in your heart.

Reach high, for stars lie hidden in your soul.
Dream deep, for every dream precedes the goal.
—PAMELA VAULL STARR

A Moment to Reflect

The dream God places in your heart is his gift, his investment in your future. It is the hope and the promise of what God knows you can become. Without that dream, you would stumble through life, unaware of your potential and purpose. The key is knowing that your dream is God's will.

Go to him often, push the distractions away and as you rest in his presence, let him open up your eyes to glimpse what is yet to be. It will renew your strength and determination to reach your goal and become the very best person you can be.

When the dream in our heart is one that God has planted there, a strange happiness flows into us. At that moment all of the spiritual resources of the universe are released to help us. Our praying is then at one with the will of God and becomes a channel for the Creator's always joyous, triumphant purposes for us and our world.

—CATHERINE WOOD MARSHALL

13

Where there is no vision, the people perish.
Proverbs 29:18 KJV

A Moment to Refresh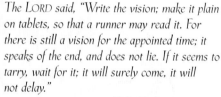

The LORD said, "Write the vision; make it plain on tablets, so that a runner may read it. For there is still a vision for the appointed time; it speaks of the end, and does not lie. If it seems to tarry, wait for it; it will surely come, it will not delay."

Habakkuk 2:2–3 NRSV

The LORD said to Jeremiah, "Call to me and I will answer you and tell you great and unsearchable things you do not know. "

Jeremiah 33:3 NIV

Paul said to the saints in Ephesus: I pray also that the eyes of your heart may be enlightened in order that you may know the hope to which he has called you, the riches of his glorious inheritance in the saints.

Ephesians 1:18 NIV

Vision is the art of seeing things invisible.

—Jonathan Swift

We fix our eyes not on what is seen, but on what is unseen. For what is seen is temporary, but what is unseen is eternal.
2 Corinthians 4:18 NIV

"I know the plans I have for you," declares the LORD, "plans to prosper you and not to harm you, plans to give you hope and a future."
Jeremiah 29:11 NIV

Let us fix our eyes on Jesus, the author and perfecter of our faith, who for the joy set before him endured the cross, scorning its shame, and sat down at the right hand of the throne of God.
Hebrews 12:2 NIV

I press on toward the goal to win the prize for which God has called me heavenward in Christ Jesus.
Philippians 3:14 NIV

To accomplish great things, we must not only act, but also dream; not only plan, but also believe.

—Anatole France

Laughing Out Loud

A Moment to Pause

Your resolve to keep on studying sinks fast when you find yourself in the middle of a marathon study session, bearing down on the books and working hard. You realize your mind has gone numb. The easiest option is simply to go to bed. But if that's out of the question—and it too often is—there is another solution. Close your eyes, focus on a humorous thought, and work yourself up to a good, loud belly laugh.

Don't hold back—think of the last time you saw a funny movie and laughed out loud. Let yourself giggle, chuckle, guffaw, gasp breathlessly. (If you have a roommate, it might be a good idea to give some warning—and a little explanation might help.) Let your original humorous thoughts give way to others. Make faces at yourself in the mirror. Practice telling the last good joke you heard. Laugh at the absurdities of life. Laugh at yourself. But laugh. Laugh until the tears come. Laugh until you feel the tiredness fleeing and your mind reviving.

Your laughter works like a steam valve on a pressure cooker. It releases tension in your muscles and rushes oxygen throughout your system, stimulating your nervous system and awakening dozing brain cells. Laughter works as a natural stimulant, lifting your mood and brightening your outlook.

Laughter is the most beautiful and beneficial
therapy God ever granted humanity.
—CHARLES R. SWINDOLL

A Moment to Reflect

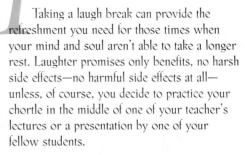

Taking a laugh break can provide the refreshment you need for those times when your mind and soul aren't able to take a longer rest. Laughter promises only benefits, no harsh side effects—no harmful side effects at all—unless, of course, you decide to practice your chortle in the middle of one of your teacher's lectures or a presentation by one of your fellow students.

Treat yourself often to laughter. Keep your resolve up. Use the sense of humor God has endowed you with to get you through those long days and nights of study, and release that pressure.

Everything's quiet,
except what's inside.
It's gurgling, threatening
to burst open wide.
I struggle to conquer the tickle within
But, the laugh I've tried stifling
eventually wins.

——CATHERINE ATKINSON

17

The joy of the LORD is your strength.
                                    Nehemiah 8:10 NIV

A Moment to Refresh

The cheerful heart has a continual feast.
                                    Proverbs 15:15 NIV

A cheerful heart is good medicine
                                    Proverbs 17:22 NIV

*Be happy, young man, while you are young,
and let your heart give you joy in the days of
your youth.*
                                    Ecclesiastes 11:9 NIV

*There is a time for everything, and a season for
every activity under heaven . . . a time to weep
and a time to laugh.*
                                    Ecclesiastes 3:1, 4 NIV

*Young people, enjoy your youth. Be happy while
you are still young.*
                                    Ecclesiastes 11:9 GNT

Laughter can relieve tension, soothe the pain of disappointment, and strengthen the spirit for the formidable tasks that always lie ahead.

—DWIGHT D. EISENHOWER

Make a joyful noise unto the LORD, all ye lands. Serve the LORD with gladness: come before his presence with singing.
Psalm 100:1–2 KJV

You have made known to me the path of life; you will fill me with joy in your presence, with eternal pleasures at your right hand.
Psalm 16:11 NIV

I have told you this so that my joy may be in you and that your joy may be complete.
John 15:11 NIV

May the righteous be glad and rejoice before God; may they be happy and joyful.
Psalm 68:3 NIV

Laughter is the closest thing to the grace of God.

—KARL BARTH

A Song for Your Soul

A Moment to Pause   What's your favorite inspirational CD? Why not set everything else aside, go someplace where you can be alone, and put it on. Don't pick up a book or concern yourself with that upcoming test. Just close your eyes and relax. Immerse yourself in the music, feeling it lift and settle, build and ebb. Focus on what you're hearing until you can move beyond the lyrics to the notes, the melody, and the rhythm.

If you're like most students, music isn't something you just listen to. You have it on while you're studying and while you're contemplating studying; you have it on while you're getting ready in the morning or while you're walking or driving to school. Music is a soundtrack for your life. But music has the power to be more—it can slow you down and refresh you.

Move beyond the music to God—its Creator. Consider that he is also enjoying the intricacies and power of the piece, right there by your side. Thank him for his wonderful gift and the restoration it is bringing to your soul.

Music is already a part of your life, let it become more—a tool to help you tune in to God.

Sing a new song to the LORD! Sing to the LORD,
all the world! Sing to the LORD, and praise him!
—PSALM 96:1–2 GNT

A Moment to Reflect

Music is much more than something to be played in the background of your life. It is the language of the soul, capable of communicating deep feelings that you're unable to express in words.

Think about allowing music to play a different role in your life as a student—quieting your mind, body, and spirit as you prepare to focus on a particular subject or take a big test. Let music draw you closer to God and set aside a special time to do this: just you, him, and the language of music. Grow ever closer to God as you open up your heart to him.

Next to theology I give to music the highest place and honor. Music is the art of the prophets, the only art that can calm the agitations of the soul; it is one of the most magnificent and delightful presents God has given us.

—MARTIN LUTHER

Is anyone happy? Let him sing songs of praise.

James 5:13 NIV

A Moment to Refresh

Let us come before him with thanksgiving and extol him with music and song. For the LORD is the great God, the great King above all gods.

Psalm 95:2–3 NIV

Let the word of Christ dwell in you richly in all wisdom; teaching and admonishing one another in psalms and hymns and spiritual songs, singing with grace in your hearts to the Lord.

Colossians 3:16 KJV

My heart is steadfast, O God, my heart is steadfast; I will sing and make melody. Awake, my soul! Awake, O harp and lyre! I will awake the dawn.

Psalm 108:1–2 NRSV

Music, the greatest good that mortals know,
and all of heaven we have below.

⁀

—Joseph Addison

The LORD is my strength and my song; he
has become my salvation. He is my God,
and I will praise him, my father's God, and
I will exalt him.

Exodus 15:2 NIV

Shout for joy to the LORD, all the earth,
burst into jubilant song with music.

Psalm 98:4 NIV

The LORD your God is with you, he is
mighty to save. He will take great delight in
you, he will quiet you with his love, he will
rejoice over you with singing.

Zephaniah 3:17 NIV

Just as my fingers on
these keys make
music, so the
selfsame sounds on
my spirit make
music, too. Music is
feeling, then, not
sound.

⁀

—Wallace Stevens

The Divine Voice

A Moment to Pause

If you find the noise and busyness around you overwhelming, perhaps it's time to step back for a moment and find a quiet place where you can be alone. Perhaps find a shady spot under a tree where no one else is sitting. Get comfortable and close your eyes. Try to tune out everything around you. You might want to try putting in earplugs. The goal is to create a place free of visual and auditory distractions.

Most campuses are busy, noisy places filled with people. Traffic, music, people talking and laughing everywhere you look. Nevertheless, it's a spiritual restorative to find a moment to shut it all out and listen to God in the midst of it all

Listen. Not to the noises or voices around you. Not to the beating of your heart or the slow, rhythmic pulse of your breathing. Not to that nagging voice of worry in the back of your head. Go beyond all of those things to the still, quiet spot at the heart of your soul, the place where God speaks. Let him talk to you. Ask him to help you find your peace among the everyday clamor of your environment. God hears your need, and he'll speak to your heart.

Before we can hear the Divine Voice we must shut out all other voices, so that we may be able to listen.

—MARK RUTHERFORD

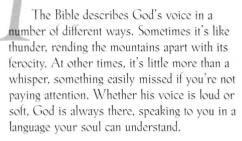

A Moment to Reflect

The Bible describes God's voice in a number of different ways. Sometimes it's like thunder, rending the mountains apart with its ferocity. At other times, it's little more than a whisper, something easily missed if you're not paying attention. Whether his voice is loud or soft, God is always there, speaking to you in a language your soul can understand.

During your soul retreat, God probably spoke many words of encouragement to you. But know that God doesn't just speak to you during quiet times. No matter what you're doing, God is always there, speaking, guiding, loving, and encouraging you. His voice is all around you. You just have to listen for it.

God is the friend of silence.
See how nature …
Trees, flowers, grass
Grow in silence.
See the stars, the moon and sun
how they move in silence.
The more we receive in silent prayer
the more we can give in our active life.
We need silence to be able to touch souls.

—AUTHOR UNKNOWN

25

God's voice thunders in marvelous ways; he
does great things beyond our understanding.
Job 37:5 NIV

A Moment to Refresh

His voice was like the roar of rushing waters,
and the land was radiant with his glory.
Ezekiel 43:2 NIV

The LORD said, "My sheep listen to my voice;
I know them, and they follow me."
John 10:27 NIV

O that today you would listen to his voice!
Psalm 95:7 NRSV

A great and strong wind rent the mountains,
and brake in pieces the rocks before the LORD;
but the LORD was not in the wind: and after
the wind an earthquake; but the LORD was not
in the earthquake: and after the earthquake a
fire; but the LORD was not in the fire: and after
the fire a still small voice.
1 Kings 19:11–12 KJV

The man who serves you best is the one who is less intent on hearing from you what he wills to hear than on shaping his will according to what he hears from you.

~

—SAINT AUGUSTINE OF HIPPO

Keep not thou silence, O God: hold not thy peace, and be not still, O God.
Psalm 83:1 KJV

To God belong wisdom and power; counsel and understanding are his.
Job 12:13 NIV

Speak, LORD, for your servant is listening.
1 Samuel 3:9 NIV

Go near and listen to all that the LORD our God says. Then tell us whatever the LORD our God tells you. We will listen and obey.
Deuteronomy 5:27 NIV

He who listens to a life-giving rebuke will be at home among the wise.
Proverbs 15:31 NIV

The Word of Christ is the great stabilizer of our lives. Listening to him leads us into truth and freedom.

~

—KLAUS BOCKMUEHL

One Foot at a Time

A Moment to Pause

How about this: Put down your books, step back from your computer, and put on your walking shoes. Go outside and start walking. Don't think about where you're going. Don't set a time when you have to be back. Just put one foot in front of the other.

Look around. What do you see? Take a deep breath. What do you smell? Stop and listen. What do you hear? Now listen to yourself. Is your mind starting to slow down? Is your body beginning to relax? Keep walking until they do.

Most times, walking is merely a way to get from point A to point B. You can be so intent on reaching your destination that how you get there becomes secondary. Your concern is when you get there. Along the way, you're probably not thinking about the walk. You're talking on your cell phone, listening to music— hurrying to class. Let this retreat show you a different way of walking; let your walking be intentional in its slower pace.

Think of the times you have gone for a walk just for the pleasure of it or just to relax. Perhaps you were on a nature trail in the woods or strolling along the beach with an old friend. As you walk now, remember these pleasant times of peace and relaxation.

Everywhere is walking distance if you have the time.
—STEVEN WRIGHT

A Moment to Reflect

Jesus had a stressful life. Wherever he went, he was mobbed by crowds of people begging him to heal them, deliver them, or teach them about God. The only way he could get a moment's peace was to walk away and spend time alone with God. Jesus knew that with the pressure of everyday life, spending time alone was an absolute necessity. Walking was a great way to do this.

Are you struggling with a difficult problem? Worried about an upcoming assignment? Follow Jesus' example: When the pressure mounts, set everything aside and go for a walk. Lay your cares before God as you stride along. More likely than not, by the time you return you'll have found the peace and assurance you're looking for.

I went out walking with my Lord.
I went walking, cares in hand.
He took my cares,
made them his own.
Sent me home with empty hands.
I went walking, full of doubt.
He took my doubts
and made things clear.
Now I walk with not a fear.

—D. A. CATHCART

*Keep my steps steady according to your
promise, and never let iniquity have dominion
over me.*

Psalm 119:133 NRSV

A Moment to Refresh

*Because so many people were coming and going
that they did not even have a chance to eat,
Jesus said to them, 'Come with me by
yourselves to a quiet place and get some rest.'*

Mark 6:31 NIV

*Saith the LORD, Stand ye in the ways, and see,
and ask for the old paths, where is the good
way, and walk therein, and ye shall find rest for
your souls.*

Jeremiah 6:16 KJV

*He has showed you, O man, what is good. And
what does the LORD require of you? To act
justly and to love mercy and to walk humbly
with your God.*

Micah 6:8 NIV

*Don't hurry, don't worry. You're only here for a short visit. So be
sure to stop and smell the flowers.*

⟡

—WALTER C. HAGEN

After sending the people away, he went up
on a hill by himself to pray. When evening
came, Jesus was there alone.

Matthew 14:23 GNT

The steps of a good man are ordered by the
LORD: and he delighteth in his way. Though
he fall, he shall not be utterly cast down: for
the LORD upholdeth him with his hand.

Psalm 37:23–24 KJV

Test me, O LORD, and try me, examine my
heart and my mind; for your love is ever
before me, and I walk continually in your
truth.

Psalm 26:2–3 NIV

*Walking around in
the park
Should feel better
than work:
The lake, the
sunshine,
The grass to lie on.*

⟡

—PHILIP LARKIN

Warm, Rich Rays

A Moment to Pause   Go out and enjoy the sun right now. Find a nice patch of grass to sit on or a bench by a patch of flowers. Look around. Notice how the sun's rays seem to bring out the beauty in everything. The sky. The trees. The people walking by, engaged in conversation. The girl playing catch with her dog. The boy zipping along on his scooter.

Now close your eyes, lie back, and drink in the sun's warmth. Imagine that the sun is God shining his love down upon you. Soothing you. Healing you. Cleansing you. Abandon yourself to the moment and soak it all up.

As you sit inside watching sunbeams slant across the grass and sidewalks, imagine soaking up the rays on the beach, by the pool, in a mountain meadow, or in a sidewalk café. It's only natural to be drawn to the sun. The sun gives you life. It also warms you and cheers you up when you're feeling down. As long as you're careful to protect your skin and eyes from overexposure, the sun can be an important friend.

This retreat is worth repeating as often as it is practical; even ten minutes a day will arm your spirit. Enjoy God's gift of the sun.

From the rising of the sun to its setting the
name of the LORD is to be praised.
—PSALM 113:3 NRSV

A Moment to Reflect

One of the most amazing things about the sun is its constancy. Day or night, cloudy or sunny, it is always there. It's been there since the beginning of time, and it'll be there until the end.

In the same way, God is always there, he is always with you, even when problems temporarily cloud your view. Find moments in your day just to sit and enjoy the warmth of his presence. It is there you will gain strength, insight, and inspiration. Just as time in the sun is good for your physical health, time with God brings sunshine to your soul.

As I lie here in bed
watching the sun break through my window
with its golden spears,
I think how strange it is
that a whirling ball of fiery gases
millions of miles away in cold, empty space
could lend so much cheer to my heart.
Must be a God thing.

—KEVIN MILLER

He makes his sun to shine on bad and good
people alike.

Matthew 5:45 GNT

A Moment to Refresh

The sun has one kind of splendor, the moon
another and the stars another; and star differs
from star in splendor.

1 Corinthians 15:41 NIV

The LORD is thy keeper: the LORD is thy shade
upon thy right hand. The sun shall not smite
thee by day, nor the moon by night.

Psalm 121:5–6 KJV

No one can look at the sun, bright as it is in the
skies after the wind has swept them clean.

Job 37:21 NIV

From the rising of the sun to the place where it
sets, the name of the LORD is to be praised.

Psalm 113:3 NIV

*Busy old fool, unruly sun, why dost thou thus, through windows
and through curtains call on us?*

ﾐ

—JOHN DONNE

He will make your righteousness shine like
the dawn, the justice of your cause like the
noonday sun.

Psalm 37:6 NIV

Praise ye him, sun and moon: praise him,
all ye stars of light.

Psalm 148:3 KJV

*The sunshine is a
glorious birth.*

ﾐ

—WILLIAM
WORDSWORTH

The city does not need the sun or the moon
to shine on it, for the glory of God gives it
light, and the Lamb is its lamp.

Revelation 21:23 NIV

The Mighty One, God, the LORD, speaks
and summons the earth from the rising of
the sun to the place where it sets.

Psalm 50:1 NIV

Shooting Hoops

A Moment to Pause   Sit back and engage your imagination. Form a mental image of your body in peak physical condition— the way God intended it to be. Imagine yourself running, lifting weights, playing a team sport, doing sit-ups and push-ups. Check out your muscle tone. Feel your muscle groups getting stronger. Listen to your heart pounding in your ears. Feel the exhilaration as your body moves and reacts like a well-oiled machine. Cool down. Stretch. Relax.

In the midst of all your exams and assignments, your social life and your extracurricular activities, you may be reluctant to take time for exercise. Especially since you're at school and your main focus is on developing your mind. Studying entails a lot of sitting around, however, and your poor body may be sorely neglected. Think about it. Your mind is a key part of your body. And if your body isn't fit, your mind won't be either. So make a point of finding a balance between exercising the brain and exercising the body.

Thank God for a healthy body. Then take the first step toward making what you have just imagined a reality. Promise yourself to walk, run, lift, sit-up, push-up, and keep that gift from God in good shape.

Those who think they have not time for bodily
exercise will sooner or later have to
find time for illness.
—*EDWARD STANLEY*

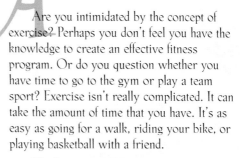

A Moment to Reflect

Are you intimidated by the concept of exercise? Perhaps you don't feel you have the knowledge to create an effective fitness program. Or do you question whether you have time to go to the gym or play a team sport? Exercise isn't really complicated. It can take the amount of time that you have. It's as easy as going for a walk, riding your bike, or playing basketball with a friend.

The key is to make exercise as enjoyable as possible so that it become something you can look forward to. When you return to your studies, you'll enjoy the feeling of being refreshed, and you'll look forward to your next workout.

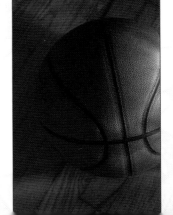

Better to hunt in fields, for health unbought,
Than fee the doctor for a nauseous drought.
The wise, for cure, on exercise depend;
God never made his work, for man to mend.

ᔓ

—JOHN DRYDEN

An athlete who runs in a race cannot win the prize unless he obeys the rules.

2 Timothy 2:5 GNT

A Moment to Refresh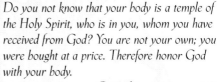

Do you not know that your body is a temple of the Holy Spirit, who is in you, whom you have received from God? You are not your own; you were bought at a price. Therefore honor God with your body.

1 Corinthians 6:19–20 NIV

I harden my body with blows and bring it under complete control, to keep myself from being disqualified after having called other to the contest.

1 Corinthians 9:27 GNT

I have fought a good fight, I have finished my course, I have kept the faith: henceforth there is laid up for me a crown of righteousness, which the Lord, the righteous judge, shall give me at that day: and not to me only, but unto all them also that love his appearing.

2 Timothy 4:7–8 KJV

Look to your health; and if you have it, praise God, and value it next to a good conscience; for health is the second blessing that we mortals are capable of; a blessing that money can't buy.

—IZAAK WALTON

Keep yourself in training for a godly life. Physical exercise has some value, but spiritual exercise is valuable in every way, because it promises life both for the present and for the future.

1 Timothy 4:7–8 GNT

Since we are surrounded by such a great cloud of witnesses, let us throw off everything that hinders and the sin that so easily entangles, and let us run with perseverance the race marked out for us.

Hebrews 12:1 NIV

Do you not know that in a race all the runners run, but only one gets the prize? Run in such a way as to get the prize.

1 Corinthians 9:24 NIV

A poet is a nightingale, who sits in darkness and sings to cheer its own solitude with sweet sounds.

—PERCY BYSSHE SHELLEY

Lively Lines

A Moment to Pause   Pick up a book of poetry and choose a poem, or pick up your Bible and choose a psalm to read. Poetry has been called the highest form of communication—moving into the mind and beyond to the soul. That's because poetry is all about painting pictures with words. These images burn themselves into your mind, creating feelings and impressions that stick with you. No wonder God included them in the Bible. They provide a powerful way to communicate his message of love.

Read your selection through silently to get the gist of it. Then read it again out loud. This time, meditate on the images presented. What thoughts or feelings do they evoke? Now read your selection one more time out loud, listening for the rhythm and the harmony of the words.

Now try writing a poem of your own. Make it an exercise for your soul's sake. Write about anything you want: nature, God, love. Just be sure that your topic moves you spiritually and emotionally and is something you feel passionate about. Express the deepest feelings in your heart. Let your poetry express what you feel deep down inside—a bit of beauty, yours to keep.

If bread is the first necessity of life, recreation is
a close second.
—*Edward Bellamy*

A Moment to Reflect

The Psalms paint some wonderful images of God and his relationship to humankind. They have inspired countless books, poems, paintings, and other works of art. Your life can be greatly enriched by making the Psalms—or any other poetry—a regular part of your day. Good starting points include: Psalms 1, 18, 23, 30, 111, 123, and 139.

If you're interested in reading some good inspirational poetry, try going to the library and finding a book by John Donne, a Christian poet from the seventeenth century. Other Christian poets to check out include John Milton, William Wordsworth, William Blake, and Percy Bysshe Shelley. Use the works of any one of them as a basis for future soul retreats.

When power leads man toward arrogance, poetry reminds him of his limitations. When power narrows the areas of man's concern, poetry reminds him of the richness and diversity of his existence. When power corrupts, poetry cleanses, for art establishes the basic human truths, which must serve as the touchstone of our judgment.

—John Fitzgerald Kennedy

Does not the ear test words as the tongue tastes food?

Job 12:11 NIV

A Moment to Refresh

My heart is stirred by a noble theme as I recite my verses for the king; my tongue is the pen of a skillful writer.

Psalm 45:1 NIV

How sweet are thy words unto my taste! yea, sweeter than honey to my mouth!

Psalm 119:103 KJV

Pleasant words are like a honeycomb, sweetness to the soul and health to the body.

Proverbs 16:24 NRSV

The LORD is my strength and my song; he has become my salvation. He is my God, and I will praise him, my father's God, and I will exalt him.

Exodus 15:2 NIV

Poetry is simply the most beautiful, impressive and widely effective mode of saying things, and hence its importance.

ॐ

—MATTHEW ARNOLD

Speak to one another with the words of
psalms, hymns, and sacred songs; sing
hymns and psalms to the Lord with praise
in your hearts.
Ephesians 5:19 GNT

The words of the wise are like goads, their
collected sayings like firmly embedded
nails—given by one Shepherd.
Ecclesiastes 12:11 NIV

God is the King of all the earth; sing to him
a psalm of praise.
Psalm 47:7 NIV

Hear this, you kings! Listen, you rulers! I
will sing to the LORD, I will sing; I will
make music to the LORD, the God of Israel.
Judges 5:3 NIV

*Poetry is the mother
tongue of mankind.*

ॐ

—JOHAN GEORG
HAMANN

Life's Treasures

A Moment to Pause Take time to stop and reflect on the friendships you enjoy. Think about the friends who sit by you in class, share their study notes when you're out sick, pick you up when you need a ride, stand up for you when it counts. Ask yourself how your friends have influenced your life. Consider what they have taught you and how they have encouraged you. Think about some of the fun experiences that you have shared.

Friendship is one of the most delightful treasures in life—a true gift from God. So when you encounter friendship, do everything you can to preserve it. As you reach out in friendship, you will discover fresh insights, enlarged perspective, renewed hope, and emotional reinforcement.

As you think of each friend, pray for that person, thanking God for his or her special qualities. Then ask God to help you show each person how much you appreciate him or her. Does one of your friends need a word of encouragement, a study partner, an honest compliment, a shoulder to cry on? As you recognize each friend's need, make a note to do what you can to fill that need

According to the Bible, human beings weren't designed to exist alone. What a delightful privilege it is to need one another.

To have a good friend is one of the highest delights of life.
—Author Unknown

A Moment to Reflect

*I*f you read about the lives of famous and influential people, you will soon discover that most of them have benefited from the help of a close group of friends who encouraged them, critiqued them, supported them, and otherwise contributed to their lives along the way. This is true of writers, teachers, politicians, artists, and business leaders.

You probably want to achieve something great in life too. Make sure your friends are the kind of people who will encourage you to keep pursuing your goals. And make sure you're the same sort of friend to do the same for them.

From quiet homes and first beginning,
Out to the undiscovered ends,
There's nothing worth the wear of winning,
But laughter and the love of friends.

—HILLAIRE BELLOC

Friends always show their love. What are
relatives for if not to share trouble?

Proverbs 17:17 GNT

A Moment to Refresh

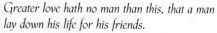

Greater love hath no man than this, that a man
lay down his life for his friends.

John 15:13 KJV

Perfume and incense bring joy to the heart, and
the pleasantness of one's friend springs from his
earnest counsel.

Proverbs 27:9 NIV

Two are better than one, because they have a
good return for their work: If one falls down,
his friend can help him up.

Ecclesiastes 4:9–10 NIV

God is to be trusted, the God who called you to
have fellowship with his Son Jesus Christ, our
Lord.

1 Corinthians 1:9 GNT

One friend in a lifetime is much; two are many; three are hardly possible.

❧

—HENRY BROOKS ADAMS

Wounds from a friend can be trusted, but
an enemy multiplies kisses.
Proverbs 27:6 NIV

A righteous man is cautious in friendship,
but the way of the wicked leads them astray.
Proverbs 12:26 NIV

Some friends play at friendship but a true
friend sticks closer than one's nearest kin.
Proverbs 18:24 NRSV

The Elder wrote to Gaius: My dear friend,
you are so faithful in the work you do for
other Christians, even when they are
strangers. They have spoken to the church
here about your love.
3 John 1:5–6 GNT

The impulse of love that leads us to the doorway of a friend is the voice of God within and we need not be afraid to follow it.

❧

—AGNES SANFORD

Catching Some Z's

A Moment to Pause Clear the books off your bed, turn out the lights, and lie down. Forget about your studies for a while. Just close your eyes and lie still until your mind is quiet. Starting with your toes and working upward, consciously will each part of your body to relax. And then, let yourself just quietly drift off . . . to sleep.

When obligations and activities overflow and you burn the midnight oil, sleep is usually the big loser. Maybe you stay up all night cramming for an exam. Or maybe you are one of those people who are "inspired by pressure" and find yourself putting off term papers until the night before they're due.

Researchers have discovered that during sleep, your brain processes the information you stuffed into your head while you were awake. This means that sleep actually causes your brain to work more effectively, boosting creativity and increasing memory. This principle is similar to a computer (your brain) that works offline (in your sleep) to process a backlog of data. Think of sleep as an integral part of the learning process, and make sure you get the amount your body needs. Regular sleep retreats will help you stay at your best.

It is in vain that you rise up early and go late to rest, eating the bread of anxious toil; for God gives sleep to his beloved.
—*PSALM 127:2 NRSV*

A Moment to Reflect

God's plan for success in school and in life includes a balanced lifestyle, one that promotes a healthy response in your body, your mind, and your spirit. That means pacing yourself in regard to study, work, recreation, and, of course, sleep. Going overboard in any area will cause the others to suffer. Ultimately, you will lose more than you gain.

Take time to evaluate your activities. Are you carrying too many subjects? If you're working, are you trying to get in too many hours? How many hours of sleep do you get on an average night? Experts suggest getting at least eight—a good goal to pursue.

Come, Sleep! O Sleep, the certain knot of peace,
The baiting-place of wit, the balm of woe,
The poor man's wealth, the prisoner's release,
Th'indifferent judge between the high and low.

—Sir Philip Sidney

49

*My heart is glad, and my soul rejoices; my
body also rests secure.*

Psalm 16:9 NRSV

A Moment to Refresh

*The sleep of a laborer is sweet, whether he eats
little or much.*

Ecclesiastes 5:12 NIV

*Jesus said, "Come to me, all you who are weary
and burdened, and I will give you rest. Take my
yoke upon you and learn from me, for I am
gentle and humble in heart, and you will find
rest for your souls."*

Matthew 11:28–30 NIV

*When I lie down, I go to sleep in peace; you
alone, O LORD, keep me perfectly safe.*

Psalm 4:8 GNT

*God gives strength to the weary and increases
the power of the weak.*

Isaiah 40:9 NIV

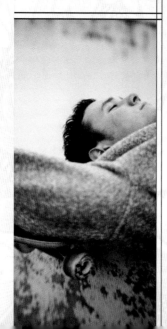

Don't count sheep if you can't sleep. Talk to the shepherd.

—PAUL FROST

On the seventh day God finished the work that he had done, and he rested on the seventh day from all the work that he had done.

Genesis 2:2 NRSV

The LORD said to Moses, "Six days shall work be done, but the seventh day is a sabbath of solemn rest, holy to the LORD.

Exodus 31:15 NRSV

My soul finds rest in God alone; my salvation comes from him.

Psalm 62:1 NIV

Those who hope in the LORD will renew their strength.

Isaiah 40:31 NIV

One hour's sleep before midnight is worth three after.

—GEORGE HERBEST

Through the Pages

A Moment to Pause   With book in hand, curl up on a sunny window seat, throw a blanket under a tree and stretch out, or lean back in a favorite easy chair. Prepare to lose yourself in the book's pages. As a student, you do your share of reading—most classes have a mountain of reading materials to work through—but reading for pleasure is often an entirely different experience.

Reading for pleasure provides rest, restoration, and inspiration for the mind. It's a good idea to have on hand at least one book that you have chosen for that purpose. It might be a book of poetry, a book of light humor, or a book filled with beautiful images. Perhaps you would like reading the story of some true life event, a classic novel filled with adventure and intrigue (*Treasure Island* and *Moby Dick* are good choices), or a book that draws you into a deeper relationship with God.

As you begin your book, follow the characters to foreign lands, laugh out loud, soak up the beauty in the words and images. Read slowly in order to relish each plot development or wise insight. Stay in your literary wonderland as long as possible. And when your retreat has to end, put a marker in your book to remind you to visit it again soon.

In all things I sought quiet; and found it not
save in retirement and in books.

—THOMAS À KEMPIS

A Moment to Reflect

When you sign up for a new course, you are usually given a reading list of books that are either required or recommended for getting the most out of class. Think about creating a reading list of your own that comprises books and other publications that you would like to read for pleasure.

Be sure the Bible is on your list. That amazing book has much to offer the casual reader as well as the dedicated student. It contains drama, humor, poetry, and high adventure. It also serves as a blueprint for establishing an exciting and unique relationship with God.

Books, books, and still more books:
stacked on floors, on chairs, in nooks,
crammed with friends and foes alike,
wound thick with yarns from days gone by.
So many avenues still to explore,
And every cover, an open door.

—D. A. CATHCART

Pleasant words are a honeycomb, sweet to the soul and healing to the bones.

Proverbs 16:24 NIV

A Moment to Refresh

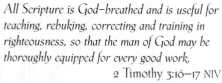

All Scripture is God-breathed and is useful for teaching, rebuking, correcting and training in righteousness, so that the man of God may be thoroughly equipped for every good work.

2 Timothy 3:16–17 NIV

Everything that was written in the past was written to teach us, so that through endurance and the encouragement of the Scriptures we might have hope.

Romans 15:4 NIV

Happy is the one who reads this book, and happy are those who listen to the words of this prophetic message and obey what is written in this book!

Revelation 1:3 GNT

Reading is to the mind what exercise is to the body.

—SIR RICHARD STEELE

My eyes stay open through the watches of the night, that I may meditate on your promises.

Psalm 119:148 NIV

The wise in heart are called discerning, and pleasant words promote instruction.

Proverbs 16:21 NIV

Philip ran up to the chariot and heard the man reading Isaiah the prophet. "Do you understand what you are reading?" Philip asked. "How can I," he said, "unless someone explains it to me?" So he invited Philip to come up and sit with him.

Acts 8:30 NIV

A book is like a garden carried in the pocket.

—ANCIENT PROVERB

A Cool Drink

A Moment to Pause Close your eyes and imagine this: You've been trekking through the desert for days. You're lost. You're parched. Your lips are cracked, and your tongue is swollen. Suddenly you spot something in the distance. At first, you think it's a mirage. But as you draw closer, you see trees and green grass. Then a familiar sparkle catches your eye. You can't believe it. Water! You dash forward and dive right in, immersing yourself in its cool, life-giving embrace. Imagine how it tastes, how it feels.

Now indulge for real. Head for the kitchen and pour yourself a tall glass of cool, clear water. Drink it slowly. As you do, imagine yourself being refreshed, each cell soaking up its portion of water's abundant benefits. Hold a little in your mouth. Feel it wash over your teeth and your tongue. Then as you swallow, imagine that the water cleansing and renewing everything it touches. Whisper a prayer of thanks to God for this life-preserving liquid.

Water is an amazing substance. It hydrates your body more effectively than soda, juice, coffee, tea, or any other drink. As you run from class to class pursuing your busy schedule, make sure you get as much as possible of this replenishing drink.

*With joy you will draw water from
the wells of salvation.*
—ISAIAH 12:3 NRSV

A Moment to Reflect

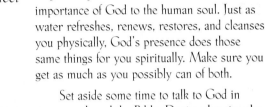

Water is so important to the body that the biblical writers often used it to describe the importance of God to the human soul. Just as water refreshes, renews, restores, and cleanses you physically, God's presence does those same things for you spiritually. Make sure you get as much as you possibly can of both.

Set aside some time to talk to God in prayer and read the Bible. During that time let him refresh and renew your soul. Take every opportunity you can find to meet with God—the Living Water—each day. It will bring life to your body, your soul, and your spirit.

Every morning the sun rises to warm the earth. If it were to fail to shine for just one minute, all life on the earth would die. The rains come to water the earth. There is fertility in the soil, life in the seeds, oxygen in the air. The providence of God is about us in unbelievable abundance every moment. But so often we just take it for granted.

—*Charles L. Allen*

Jesus said, "Whoever believes in me, as the Scripture has said, streams of living water will flow from within him."

John 7:38 NIV

A Moment to Refresh

I will pour water on the thirsty land, and streams on the dry ground; I will pour out my Spirit on your offspring, and my blessing on your descendants.

Isaiah 44:3 NIV

Jesus said, "You can be sure that whoever gives even a drink of cold water to one of the least of these my followers because he is my follower, will certainly receive his reward."

Matthew 10:42 GNT

As the deer pants for streams of water, so my soul pants for you, O God.

Psalm 42:1 NIV

The best thing to do with water is to use a lot of it.

—Philip Johnson

O God, thou art my God; early will I seek thee: my soul thirsteth for thee, my flesh longeth for thee in a dry and thirsty land, where no water is.

Psalm 63:1 KJV

Jesus said, "I am the bread of life. Whoever comes to me will never be hungry, and whoever believes in me will never be thirsty."

John 6:35 NRSV

Jesus said, "If you only knew what God gives you and who it is that is asking you for a drink, you would ask him, and he would give you life-giving water."

John 4:10 GNT

When drinking water, don't forget who dug the well.

—Ancient Proverb

The Written Word

A Moment to Pause
The Bible is filled with wonderful wisdom and glorious promises. Use a red-letter Bible if you have one. If your personal Bible is a black-letter edition, check the literature section of your school library to borrow a red-letter edition. Open to the New Testament and find a passage set in red type. The red letters indicate the words attributed to Jesus while he was here on earth. John 14 is a wonderful place to start.

In a quiet, comfortable place, choose a red-letter passage and read it slowly and purposefully several times. Close your eyes and meditate on the words. Imagine Jesus speaking them to you directly. Picture the expression on his face. What do you think his voice would sound like? What do you see in his eyes? Do you understand his words more than if you simply read them? Feel the warmth of his presence. Let it all soak in.

What you visualized is more than just a happy illusion. The Bible really does contain Jesus' words, and they were written to you and to all humankind. When you read Jesus' words, God is right there, loving and caring for you. Jesus' words are timeless. When your retreat is over, take them with you.

*The unfolding of your words gives light; it
imparts understanding to the simple.*
—PSALM 119:130 NRSV

A Moment to Reflect

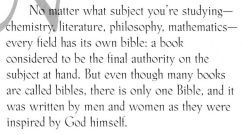

No matter what subject you're studying—chemistry, literature, philosophy, mathematics—every field has its own bible: a book considered to be the final authority on the subject at hand. But even though many books are called bibles, there is only one Bible, and it was written by men and women as they were inspired by God himself.

Regular Bible reading is essential for growing closer to God and gaining a better understanding of his purpose for your life. So if you want to make the most of who you are, make a habit of retreating into this book again and again.

God did not write a book and send it by messenger to be read at a distance by unaided minds. He spoke a Book and lives in His spoken words, constantly speaking His words and causing the power of them to persist across the years.

—A. W. TOZER

The grass withereth, the flower fadeth: but the word of our God shall stand for ever.

Isaiah 40:8 KJV

A Moment to Refresh

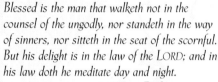

Blessed is the man that walketh not in the counsel of the ungodly, nor standeth in the way of sinners, nor sitteth in the seat of the scornful. But his delight is in the law of the LORD; and in his law doth he meditate day and night.

Psalm 1:1–2 KJV

Jesus said, "Man does not live on bread alone, but on every word that comes from the mouth of God."

Matthew 4:4 NIV

Do not let this Book of the Law depart from your mouth; meditate on it day and night, so that you may be careful to do everything written in it. Then you will be prosperous and successful.

Joshua 1:8 NIV

When the Bible speaks, God speaks.

—*B. B. WARFIELD*

Jesus said, "Heaven and earth will pass away, but my words will never pass away."
Matthew 24:35 NIV

Your word is a lamp to my feet and a light for my path.
Psalm 119:105 NIV

I have hidden your word in my heart that I might not sin against you.
Psalm 119:11 NIV

All Scripture is inspired by God and is useful for teaching the truth, rebuking error, correcting faults, and giving instruction for right living, so that the person who serves God may be fully equipped to do every kind of good deed.
2 Timothy 3:16–17 GNT

The Scriptures and the words of Jesus possess a terrible power in themselves and a wonderful sweetness.

—*JUSTIN MARTYR*

Moving Your Feet

A Moment to Pause
What kind of music do you like? Classical, inspirational, rock, jazz, Christian? Close the door, turn on the radio, or put on one of your favorite CDs. Let the music rock your soul. Move your feet, glide and twist, sway and spin. Let your body move to the rhythm. If there are words, sing along, if not, make up your own. Dance to the music—loosen your tired muscles, release your weariness, let yourself go.

Now find a comfortable place and enjoy the music in another way. Listen to the words of the songs. Think about what they're saying to you. See if you can imagine what the lyricist was trying to communicate when he or she penned the words. What emotions do you think that person was expressing? If you've chosen to listen to classical music, close your eyes and let your imagination wander with the dynamics—what is the mood? What do you see? What is happening?

What about God—the creator of the music you enjoy so much? As your musical soul retreat comes to an end, whisper a prayer of thanks to him for all ways music has made a difference in your life.

Music is for the soul what wind is for the ship, blowing her onwards in the direction in which she is steered.

WILLIAM BOOTH

A Moment to Reflect

An ancient Chinese emperor was unable to travel across his vast kingdom due to illness. Instead, he had each province send in a musician so he could hear the songs each province was producing. By listening to the music, the emperor believed he could tell how each province was doing. If the music was joyous, he knew things were going well. If it was melancholy and sad, he knew something was wrong.

As the emperor wisely observed, the music you enjoy is a good measure of the state of your soul. Think about the kinds of music you like. What do they say about your soul?

There is sweet music here that softer falls
Than petals from blown roses on the grass,
Or night-dews on still waters between walls
Of shadowy granite, in a gleaming pass;
Music that gentler on the spirit lies,
Than tired eyelids upon tired eyes;
Music that bring sweet sleep down from the
blissful skies.

—Alfred, Lord Tennyson

It is a good thing to give thanks unto the LORD, and to sing praises unto thy name, O most High.

Psalm 92:1 KJV

A Moment to Refresh

My heart is steadfast, O God, my heart is steadfast; I will sing and make music. Awake, my soul! Awake, harp and lyre! I will awaken the dawn. I will praise you, O Lord, among the nations; I will sing of you among the peoples.

Psalm 57:7–9 NIV

What should I do, then? I will pray with my spirit, but I will pray also with my mind; I will sing with my spirit, but I will sing also with my mind.

1 Corinthians 14:15 GNT

My heart is steadfast, O God; I will sing and make music with all my soul.

Psalm 108:1 NIV

Perhaps all music, even the newest, is not so much something discovered as something that re-emerges from where it lay buried in the memory, inaudible as a melody cut in a disc of flesh. A composer lets me hear a song that has always been shut up silent within me.

—JEAN GENET

The winter is past, the rain is over and gone. The flowers appear on the earth; the time of singing has come, and the voice of the turtledove is heard in our land.

Song of Songs 2:11–12 NRSV

He put a new song in my mouth, a hymn of praise to our God. Many will see and fear and put their trust in the LORD.

Psalm 40:3 NIV

Then I heard every creature in heaven and on earth and under the earth and on the sea, and all that is in them, singing: "To him who sits on the throne and to the Lamb be praise and honor and glory and power, for ever and ever!"

Revelation 5:13 NIV

Music has charms to soothe a savage breast, to soften rocks, or bend a knotted oak.

—WILLIAM CONGREVE

Grab a Snack

A Moment to Pause

Imagine you're up late. You've been pushing hard to finish a term paper or cram for a test. You're tired, but you've got to keep going for a while longer. Then it hits you—a small rumble in the pit of your stomach. You try to ignore it, but it keeps coming back louder each time, a constant reminder that your brain is housed in a body—and your body needs food. It is a fact that your body burns ten more calories per hour when you're studying than when you're just sitting around.

So put down what you're doing and head to the kitchen for a snack. Fix yourself something tasty and good for you. A celery stick with peanut butter and raisins. A grilled-cheese sandwich. A bowl of frozen yogurt. A piece of pizza. A handful of almonds or peanuts. An apple. Eat slowly, focusing on and enjoying each bite.

Now sit back for a minute or two longer and consider the bounty God has provided for you—a wide assortment of foods to give your body and mind a much-needed energy boost. Before you head back to the books, thank God for the snack you have just enjoyed.

Whatever satisfies hunger is good food.
—ANCIENT PROVERB

A Moment to Reflect

Just as your body needs food to keep it strong and energized, your soul needs spiritual food—time with God to talk to him in prayer and read his words from the Bible.

When you feel you need a spiritual boost, take a few minutes to find something tasty in God's Word. One verse may be enough to keep you going until your regular reading or study time. Try something like Matthew 11:28, where Jesus said, "Take my yoke upon you and learn from me, for I am gentle and humble in heart, and you will find rest for your souls" (NIV).

No fear can stand up to hunger, no patience can wear it out, disgust simply does not exist where hunger is; and as to superstition, beliefs, and what you may call principles, they are less than chaff in a breeze.

—JOSEPH CONRAD

God has given food to those who fear Him; He
will remember His covenant forever.

Psalm 111:5 NASB

A Moment to Refresh

Jesus said, "Do not be worried about the food
and drink you need in order to stay alive, or
about clothes for your body. After all, isn't life
worth more than food? And isn't the body
worth more than clothes?"

Matthew 6:25 GNT

Jesus said, "Do not work for food that spoils;
instead, work for the food that lasts for eternal
life. This is the food which the Son of Man will
give you, because God, the Father, has put his
mark of approval on him."

John 6:27 GNT

"My food," said Jesus, "is to do the will of him
who sent me and to finish his work."

John 4:34 NIV

Hunger is the best spice.

—SWEDISH PROVERB

Jesus said, "Blessed are they which do hunger and thirst after righteousness: for they shall be filled."

Matthew 5:6 KJV

Let them give thanks to the LORD for His lovingkindness, and for His wonders to the sons of men! For He has satisfied the thirsty soul, and the hungry soul He has filled with what is good.

Psalm 107:8–9 NASB

"I am the bread of life," Jesus told the people. "He who comes to me will never be hungry; those who believe in me will never be thirsty."

John 6:35 GNT

A hungry stomach cannot hear.

—JEAN DE LA FONTAINE

Perpetual Tranquility

A Moment to Pause   Animals provide a wonderful and varied service to humankind. For many animals that includes a friendly disposition and the art of companionship. If you have a pet of your own, take a break from the books for a few minutes and make a connection.

Get down at eye level and watch your goldfish scoot around its bowl. Imagine yourself entering its watery world, wiggling and diving, circling the miniature castle at the bottom of the bowl, free of responsibilities and obligations. If you have a playful pet, join in the fun. Throw a stick and run with your dog to fetch it. Run and jump until you feel invigorated and refreshed.

If you have a cat, it may be full of affection. Pull it up onto your lap and let it rest there. Rub its fur and enjoy its satisfied response. Imitate its relaxed breathing until you're feeling rested and happy yourself.

As you run your fingers through your cat's fur, thank God for the precious gift of your pet. As you watch your goldfish swimming contentedly inside its domain, thank God for the vast diversity of his creation. As you run beside your pet, thank God for the need your pet fills in your life.

All animals except man know that the principle business of life is to enjoy it.
—SAMUEL BUTLER

A Moment to Reflect

Have you ever asked yourself why your pet seems to be able to relax and have fun with such ease? Simple: It trusts God and you as his agent. Your pet is confident that what it needs will be provided in some form.

You are precious to God. He is always watching over you, providing for your needs, loving and caring and anticipating the time you spend together. Put your faith in him and trust him to provide for you—inspiration for your next paper, a good memory on your next test, your basic needs. Then, simply rest and relax in his presence

God commanded, "Let the earth produce all kinds of animal life: domestic and wild, large and small"—and it was done. So God made them all, and he was pleased with what he saw. Then God said, "And now we will make human beings; they will be like us and resemble us. They will have power over the fish, the birds, and all animals, domestic and wild, large and small."

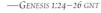

—GENESIS 1:24–26 GNT

All kinds of animals, birds, reptiles and creatures of the sea are being tamed and have been tamed by man.

James 3:7 NIV

A Moment to Refresh

Jesus said, "Are not two sparrows sold for a penny? Yet not one of them will fall to the ground apart from the will of your Father."

Matthew 10:29 NIV

The LORD said, "Every animal of the forest is mine, and the cattle on a thousand hills. I know every bird in the mountains, and the creatures of the field are mine."

Psalm 50:10–11 NIV

All kinds of animals, birds, reptiles and creatures of the sea are being tamed and have been tamed by man.

James 3:7 NIV

God said, "Let the land produce living creatures according to their kinds: livestock, creatures that move along the ground, and wild animals, each according to its kind." And it was so.

Genesis 1:24 NIV

If a dog jumps into your lap it is because he is fond of you; but if a cat does the same thing it is because your lap is warmer.

꒳

Jesus said, "Look at the crows: they don't plant seeds or gather a harvest; they don't have storage rooms or barns; God feeds them! You are worth so much more than birds!"

Luke 12:24 GNT

God . . . richly provides us with everything for our enjoyment.

1 Timothy 6:17 NIV

Who provides for the raven its prey, when its young ones cry to God, and wander about for lack of food?

Job 38:41 NRSV

God said, "Bring out every kind of living creature that is with you—the birds, the animals, and all the creatures that move along the ground—so they can multiply on the earth."

Genesis 8:16 NIV

Love the animals: God has given them the rudiments of thought and joy untroubled.

꒳

—FYODOR DOSTOEVSKY

Talking to God

A Moment to Pause   Find a private place where you won't feel inhibited, and pour out your heart to God. Talk to him aloud as if he were right there with you, which he is. Talk about your day, your week, your school work, your teachers, your classmates, your goals, your disappointments, your achievements—anything that's on your mind.

For many people, prayer is like trying to write a difficult term paper. Where should you begin, what should you include or leave out, how do you end a prayer—many people have asked these questions, so you're in plenty of company if these are your concerns.

Prayer is as straightforward and natural as opening your mouth and talking to your best friend. But unlike your best friend, God is always available and ready and willing to listen, twenty-four hours a day, seven days a week. Practice the habit of talking to God spontaneously. Something good happen? Thank you, God. A friend is in trouble? Please help her, God. Unsure how to respond? What should I do, God?

Linger for a few moments at the end of your prayer retreat, and you may hear God answer you deep inside your heart.

Prayer opens the heart to God, and it is the
means by which the soul, though empty,
is filled by God.
—JOHN BUNYAN

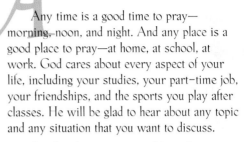

A Moment to Reflect

Any time is a good time to pray— morning, noon, and night. And any place is a good place to pray—at home, at school, at work. God cares about every aspect of your life, including your studies, your part-time job, your friendships, and the sports you play after classes. He will be glad to hear about any topic and any situation that you want to discuss.

Speak to him as you would speak to a loving father, a trusted friend, or a wise teacher, for he is all those things. Be assured that he hears and cares about every word. He welcomes your prayers about anything, anytime, anywhere.

If, when I kneel to pray,
With eager lips I say:
"Lord, give me all the things that I desire—
Health, wealth, fame, friends, brave heart,
religious fire,
The power to sway my fellow-men at will,
And strength for might works to banish ill,"—
In such a prayer as this
The blessing I just miss.

—CHARLES FRANCIS RICHARDSON

Jesus said, "If you believe, you will receive whatever you ask for in prayer."
Matthew 21:22 NIV

A Moment to Refresh

Be joyful always, pray at all times, be thankful in all circumstances. This is what God wants from you in your life in union with Christ Jesus.
1 Thessalonians 5:16–18 GNT

Pray in the Spirit on all occasions with all kinds of prayers and requests. With this in mind, be alert and always keep on praying for all the saints.
Ephesians 6:18 NIV

Confess your faults one to another, and pray one for another, that ye may be healed. The effectual fervent prayer of a righteous man availeth much.
James 5:16 KJV

In prayer the lips ne'er act the winning part, without the sweet concurrence of the heart.

ॐ

—ROBERT HERRICK

Jesus said, "When you pray, go to your room, close the door, and pray to your Father, who is unseen. And your Father, who sees what you do in private, will reward you."

Matthew 6:6 GNT

Let everyone who is godly pray to You in a time when you may be found; Surely in a flood of great waters they will not reach him.

Psalm 32:6 NASB

Jesus said, "Your Father knows what you need before you ask him."

Matthew 6:8 NIV

More things are wrought by prayer than this world dreams of.

ॐ

—ALFRED, LORD TENNYSON

Talk Up a New Friend

A Moment to Pause How much do you know about the people who live near you, sit in your classes, or go to your church? The way to find out is to simply ask. And when you do, you will probably find that a conversation follows.

Pause for a few minutes and become an observer. Take a seat in the back of the classroom or stand in an inconspicuous place in the hall. Look at the faces that come and go—many probably familiar—faces you see every day. Now focus on one of them. Is it someone you think you would be interested in knowing?

If so, take a chance. Walk up to that person, look into his or her eyes and ask how he or she likes the class or the teacher or the weather. Just ask and see what happens. Choose a question that shows your interest in that person without being too nosy. Then be persistent. If one question doesn't do it, ask another and keep asking until some give and take develops.

Conversation can be a wonderful experience, a refreshing breath of air in the midst of busy day. It can have lasting benefits as well. Conversations are where friendships are born.

A single conversation across the table with a wise man is better than ten years' study of books.
—HENRY WADSWORTH LONGFELLOW

A Moment to Reflect

Before the invention of radio and television, conversation was one of the main forms of entertainment. People would gather together in the evening after the work was done and tell stories or discuss the news of the day. Times have changed, but the pleasurable benefits of conversation have not.

Thank God for the ability he has given you to make a connection with those around you. And make that connection as often as possible with all the people in your life and all the people you would like to have in your life. It's a gift you can give to others and keep for yourself at the same time.

Conversation is but carving!
Give no more to every guest
Than he's able to digest.
Give him always of the prime,
And but little at a time.
Carve to all but just enough,
Let them neither starve nor stuff,
And that you may have your due
Let your neighbor carve for you.

—JONATHAN SWIFT

The lips of the wise protect them.
Proverbs 14:3 NIV

A Moment to Refresh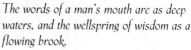

The words of a man's mouth are as deep waters, and the wellspring of wisdom as a flowing brook.
Proverbs 18:4 KJV

Those who love a pure heart and are gracious in speech will have the king as a friend.
Proverbs 22:11 NRSV

Let the words of my mouth and the meditation of my heart be acceptable in your sight, O LORD, my rock and my Redeemer.
Psalm 19:14 NASB

Moses was educated in all the wisdom of the Egyptians and was powerful in speech and action.
Acts 7:22 NIV

In conversation, humor is worth more than wit and easiness more than knowledge.

ॐ

—GEORGE HERBERT

Let your conversation be always full of grace, seasoned with salt, so that you may know how to answer everyone.
Colossians 4:6 NIV

Do not use harmful words, but only helpful words, the kind that build up and provide what is needed, so that what you say will do good to those who hear you.
Ephesians 4:29 GNT

Be an example for the believers in your speech, your conduct, your love, faith, and purity.
1 Timothy 4:12 GNT

As servants of God we commend ourselves . . . in truthful speech and in the power of God;
2 Corinthians 6:4, 7 NIV

The art of conversation is not in knowing what you ought to say, but what you ought not to say.

ॐ

—AUTHOR UNKNOWN

In Your Own Words

A Moment to Pause

Capturing your thoughts on paper can be a fascinating exercise, especially when it is for your own enlightenment and satisfaction. Set aside your assigned homework for a few minutes and let your writing hand lead you. Set a timer and give yourself five minutes to write about any topic you choose.

You may want to put into words your opinion about some topic you're discussing in class. Or maybe you would like to describe your feelings about some person you greatly admire. The subject can be anything—or it can be about trying to think of an appropriate subject and coming up with zilch.

Once you've made your choice, write freely. Writing helps you capture random impressions and images, organize them, and put them into words. This essay is for your eyes only, so write whatever you like in whatever way you like. Keep your pen moving and resist the urge to edit your writing or check your words as you go along.

When your time is up, read and reflect on what you've written. Enjoy the good feeling that comes from putting your thoughts and opinions on paper. In a sense, writing brings your thoughts to life.

Writing down your thoughts give them life and substance and immortality.
—ANDREA GARNEY

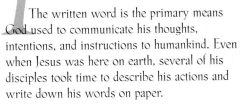

A Moment to Reflect

The written word is the primary means God used to communicate his thoughts, intentions, and instructions to humankind. Even when Jesus was here on earth, several of his disciples took time to describe his actions and write down his words on paper.

Words spoken are powerful, but words written down are durable and lasting. Through the Bible, God has given humankind a permanent message of hope and redemption. You can read his words of love any time you choose. When you do, you might want to write out a response. Let him know how you feel about what you've read.

All the words that I utter
And all the words that I write
Must spread out their wings untiring,
And never rest in their flight,
Till they come where your sad, sad heart is,
And sing to you in the night,
Beyond where the waters are moving,
Storm-darken'd or starry bright.

—WILLIAM BUTLER YEATS

You yourselves are our letter, written on your hearts, to be known and read by all.

2 Corinthians 3:2 NRSV

A Moment to Refresh

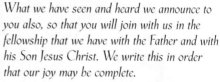

What we have seen and heard we announce to you also, so that you will join with us in the fellowship that we have with the Father and with his Son Jesus Christ. We write this in order that our joy may be complete.

1 John 1:3–4 GNT

This shall be written for the generation to come: and the people which shall be created shall praise the LORD.

Psalm 102:18 KJV

Have I not written thirty sayings for you, sayings of counsel and knowledge, teaching you true and reliable words, so that you can give sound answers to him who sent you?

Proverbs 22:20–21 NIV

To the man with an ear for verbal delicacies—the man who searches painfully for the perfect word, and puts the way of saying a thing above the thing said—there is in writing the constant joy of sudden discovery, of happy accident.

—HENRY LOUIS MENCKEN

I have written you quite boldly on some points, as if to remind you of them again, because of the grace God gave me to be a minister of Christ Jesus to the Gentiles with the priestly duty of proclaiming the gospel of God, so that the Gentiles might become an offering acceptable to God, sanctified by the Holy Spirit.

Romans 15:15–16 NIV

I have written to you, fathers, because you know Him who has been from the beginning. I have written to you, young men, because you are strong, and the word of God abides in you.

1 John 2:14 NASB

Dear friends, this is now my second letter to you. I have written both of them as reminders to stimulate you to wholesome thinking.

2 Peter 3:1 NIV

In a very real sense, the writer writes in order to teach himself.

—ALFRED KAZIN

Flight of Fancy

A Moment to Pause

It's time to step away from the books for a few minutes and stretch your imagination with some what-if questions: What if people stayed up all night working and slept all day? What if everyone moved north for the summer and south for the winter? What if you had eleven brothers and sisters? What if you went to church Monday through Friday and to school only on Sunday?

Focus on a what-if question like those above, and let your imagination run with the possibilities. Think how any of these situations would affect how you interact with your friends and family. Let your imagination lead you until you have played it out as far as you choose.

Now relax and reflect on any new insights you may have happened upon. Perhaps you may have realized that the circumstances around you would not change who you really are. Perhaps you discovered that you like a certain degree of risk and adventure in your life.

Next reflect on this question. What if . . . you opened your eyes and Jesus was standing right in front of you? Would you be happy to see him? What would you talk about? Let your imagination work on that one just as you did the others.

Perhaps imagination is only intelligence having fun.
—GEORGE SCIALABRA

A Moment to Reflect

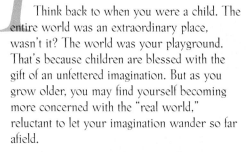

Think back to when you were a child. The entire world was an extraordinary place, wasn't it? The world was your playground. That's because children are blessed with the gift of an unfettered imagination. But as you grow older, you may find yourself becoming more concerned with the "real world," reluctant to let your imagination wander so far afield.

Imagination is another way of expressing the childlike wonder you were born with, your gift from God. God used his imagination to create the world, and retaining the freshness of a childlike imagination can enhance your potential in whatever you do.

How far, how high can we ascend
Borne upon imagination's wings?
To moon, to star, to ocean depths,
To quarks and deep atomic things.
There's no end, it seems, no unreachable height
If we but open the cage and let our dreams
take flight.

—*Kevin D. Miller*

If there be a prophet among you, I the LORD
will make myself known unto him in a vision,
and will speak unto him in a dream.

Numbers 12:6 KJV

A Moment to Refresh

It will come about after this that I will pour out
My Spirit on all mankind; And your sons and
daughters will prophesy, Your old men will
dream dreams, Your young men will see visions.

Joel 2:28 NASB

God does speak—now one way, now another—
though man may not perceive it. In a dream, in
a vision of the night, when deep sleep falls on
men as they slumber in their beds.

Job 33:14–15 NIV

To him who is able to do immeasurably more
than all we ask or imagine, according to his
power that is at work within us, to him be glory
in the church and in Christ Jesus throughout all
generations, for ever and ever!

Ephesians 3:20–21 NIV

Solitude is as needful to the imagination as society is wholesome for the character.

ॐ

—JAMES RUSSELL LOWELL

To these four young men God gave knowledge and skill in every aspect of literature and wisdom; Daniel also had insight into all visions and dreams.
Daniel 1:17 NRSV

Paul had a vision in which he saw a Macedonian standing and begging him, "Come over to Macedonia and help us!" As soon as Paul had this vision, we got ready to leave for Macedonia, because we decided that God had called us to preach the Good News to the people there.
Acts 16:9–10 GNT

He who works his land will have abundant food, but he who chases fantasies lacks judgment.
Proverbs 12:11 NIV

In the world of words, imagination is one of the forces of nature.

ॐ

—WALLACE STEVENS

From His Hand

A Moment to Pause Look around your room and make a list of everything that was given to you by someone else—from books to clothing to CDs. Your list is probably longer than you imagined. A person can be truly blessed without even realizing it. Reflect for a few moments on each item and the person who gave it to you.

Maybe the woven sea-grass rug was a gift from your mom—think about how she's blessed you with her love and care from the beginning of your life. Speak a prayer that God will bless her in return for being such a good and loving mother. Perhaps the CD player was given to you by your dad. Take a moment to reflect on your dad, how he works hard to give you food, clothing, as well as many extras. Pray that God will bless him for his commitment to provide for his family. Perhaps your best friend gave you the poster of your favorite hero. Pray that God will bless your friend and bless your friendship.

Continue down your list, thanking God for each person who has blessed your life. The next time you need a retreat for your soul, take up where you left off.

Reflect upon your present blessings, of which
every man has many.
—*Charles Dickens*

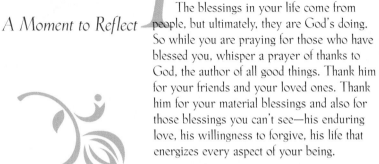

A Moment to Reflect

The blessings in your life come from people, but ultimately, they are God's doing. So while you are praying for those who have blessed you, whisper a prayer of thanks to God, the author of all good things. Thank him for your friends and your loved ones. Thank him for your material blessings and also for those blessings you can't see—his enduring love, his willingness to forgive, his life that energizes every aspect of your being.

The Bible says that your prayers of thankfulness are a blessing to him. Keep the circle of blessing moving between you and your heavenly Father.

Praise God, from whom all blessings flow!
Praise Him, all creatures here below!
Praise Him above, ye heavenly host!
Praise Father, Son, and Holy Ghost!

—THOMAS KEN

The blessing of the LORD brings wealth, and he adds no trouble to it.

Proverbs 10:22 NIV

A Moment to Refresh

Every good gift and every perfect present comes from heaven; it comes down from God, the Creator of the heavenly lights, who does not change or cause darkness by turning.

James 1:17 GNT

He that hath clean hands, and a pure heart; who hath not lifted up his soul unto vanity, nor sworn deceitfully. He shall receive the blessing from the LORD, and righteousness from the God of his salvation.

Psalm 24:4–5 KJV

Those who have faith are blessed along with Abraham, the man of faith.

Galatians 3:9 NIV

E'en crosses from his sov'reign hand are blessings in disguise.

—JAMES HERVEY

Let us give thanks to the God and Father of our Lord Jesus Christ! For in our union with Christ he has blessed us by giving us every spiritual blessing in the heavenly world.

Ephesians 1:3 GNT

Blessings are on the head of the righteous, but the mouth of the wicked conceals violence.

Proverbs 10:6 NRSV

"Bring the whole tithe into the storehouse, so that there may be food in My house, and test Me now in this," says the LORD of hosts, "if I will not open for you the windows of heaven and pour out for you a blessing until it overflows."

Malachi 3:10 NASB

'Tis expectation makes a blessing dear, heaven were not heaven, if we knew what it were.

—SIR JOHN SUCKLING

Staying In Touch

A Moment to Pause

Begin by finding a quiet place where you can write comfortably. Whom would you like to write to today? Is there someone with whom you'd like to stay in touch? Writing a letter is so satisfying. It's often easier to express yourself in writing than it is in person, and more time is available to organize your thoughts and choose the right words.

Date your letter to give it a historical context if you should read it sometime in the future. Write the person's name, and pause for a moment or two. Settle back in your chair and create a mental image of the individual. Think about what the person means to you and how he or she has affected your life. Think through what you want to say, what emotions you want to convey, what information you want to impart.

When you're happy with your mental letter, put it down on paper. Read it over to see if there is anything else you want to add. When you're satisfied, sign your name—this constitutes your affirmation that your words now say what you want them to say. When you mail your letter, you will establish a link with the person you've written to—the first step to staying in touch.

More than kisses, letters mingle souls; for thus friends absent speak.

—JOHN DONNE

A Moment to Reflect

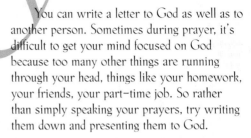

You can write a letter to God as well as to another person. Sometimes during prayer, it's difficult to get your mind focused on God because too many other things are running through your head, things like your homework, your friends, your part-time job. So rather than simply speaking your prayers, try writing them down and presenting them to God.

God loves you, and he is always glad to hear from you in any form you choose. He is interested in all the things that affect you—your problems and concerns as well as your successes and triumphs. After you finish your letter, follow up by reading something from his letter to you, the Bible.

There's no feeling better
Than receiving a letter
Handwritten and posted in the mail.
From a friend or a lover,
A child or a brother,
All serve equally well to regale.

✎

—D. A. CATHCART

Pleasant words are like a honeycomb,
sweetness to the soul and health to the body.
                                    Proverbs 16:24 NRSV

A Moment to Refresh

I have written to you briefly, exhorting and
testifying that this is the true grace of God.
                                    1 Peter 5:12 NASB

Worry can rob you of happiness, but kind
words will cheer you up.
                                    Proverbs 12:25 GNT

Bear in mind that our Lord's patience means
salvation, just as our dear brother Paul also
wrote you with the wisdom that God gave him.
He writes the same way in all his letters,
speaking in them of these matters.
                                    2 Peter 3:15–16 NIV

Mordecai sent letters to all the Jews in the 127
provinces of the kingdom of Xerxes—words of
goodwill and assurance.
                                    Esther 9:30 NIV

All letters, methinks, should be as free and easy as one's discourse, not studied as an oration, nor made up of hard words like a charm.

—DOROTHY OSBORNE

Paul wrote: When I arrive, I will give letters of introduction to the men you approve and send them with your gift to Jerusalem.

1 Corinthians 16:3 NIV

Paul wrote: I urge you by the authority of the Lord to read this letter to all the believers.

1 Thessalonians 5:27 GNT

I write these things to you who believe in the name of the Son of God, so that you may know that you have eternal life.

1 John 5:13 NRSV

I am sure, as I write this, that you will do what I ask—in fact I know that you will do even more.

Philemon 1:21 GNT

I have made this letter longer than usual, only because I have not had the time to make it shorter.

—BLAISE PASCAL

Small Indulgences

A Moment to Pause Slam shut the books and take a break for the sake of a small indulgence. It will be easier to focus on your studies when you return. God invented work, and he's also the one who came up with strawberries, chocolate, rivers, trees, and flowers. The Bible says that along with all the other gifts he's given you, he has also provided everything you need to enjoy life (1 Timothy 6:17).

Decide what small indulgence would provide a productive, satisfying respite that will lift your spirit and refresh your soul. Take a few minutes to think about how you'd like to treat yourself. Maybe you're craving a special snack, a short nap, a walk outside, a relaxing bath, or some time with your friends.

Then enjoy. Go out for a pizza or a hot fudge sundae; put a DO NOT DISTURB sign on your door and sleep for a solid hour; take a brisk walk in a nearby park, stopping occasionally to watch the squirrels play; fill up the tub and soak in the warm, luxurious water; throw a football around with your buddies. When you're finished, thank God for the ability to enjoy the life he's given you.

Enjoy pleasures, but let them be your own, and then you will taste them.
—LORD CHESTERFIELD

A Moment to Reflect

The Bible presents God in many roles, but none so compelling as that of the benevolent, loving Father who longs to provide good things for his children. Looking around at the world certainly confirms that.

God has provided everything necessary to please the senses—the breath-taking beauty of mountains, sea, and sky; the compelling sound of wind, water, and wildlife; the wonderful scent of trees, the delicate scent of flowers, and the enticing aroma of food; as well as all the other God-given pleasures of touch and taste. These things are small evidences that God wants you to take your indulgences seriously, receiving them as his gifts, and thanking him for them.

He sat inside a coffee shop
And sipped a Latin brew
While she relaxed upon the grass
And read a tale or two.
They fished for trout beside the stream
Without the slightest care
While I rushed about
For I know not what
And envied their casual air.

—ED STRAUSS

Jesus said, "I have come in order that you might have life—life in all its fullness."

John 10:10 GNT

A Moment to Refresh

My son, eat honey, for it is good, yes, the honey from the comb is sweet to your taste.

Proverbs 24:13 NASB

If you are willing and obedient, you shall eat the good of the land.

Isaiah 1:19 NRSV

Let every man prove his own work, and then shall he have rejoicing in himself alone, and not in another.

Galatians 6:4 KJV

You have made known to me the path of life; you will fill me with joy in your presence, with eternal pleasures at your right hand.

Psalm 16:11 NIV

Life admits of no delays; when pleasure can be had, it is fit to catch it. Every hour takes away part of the things that please us.

ॐ

—SAMUEL JOHNSON

Delight yourself in the LORD; *and He will give you the desires of your heart.*
Psalm 37:4 NASB

Happy are those who do not feel guilty when they do something they judge is right!
Romans 14:22 GNT

Praise the LORD. *How good it is to sing praises to our God, how pleasant and fitting to praise him!*
Psalm 147:1 NIV

Jeremiah wrote: At this I awoke and looked around. My sleep had been pleasant to me.
Jeremiah 31:26 NIV

What is this life if, full of care, we have not time to stand and stare?

ॐ

—W. H. DAVIES

Watch It Grow

A Moment to Pause Find a place near your home where you can observe a few trees up close. Examine their leaves, their branches, their bark. Look around for roots peeking out of the earth. Consider how trees draw their nutrients from the soil, the water, and the sun; how they cleanse the air by consuming carbon dioxide and producing oxygen; how bugs and birds and other creatures depend on them for life.

Jesus often used gardening to describe certain truths about God and his kingdom. For example, he used the mustard seed to describe how God's kingdom would start out small and then grow into something big. He also used wheat and weeds to illustrate how believers would be separated from nonbelievers at the end of time.

Now that you've seen how Jesus did it, come up with a few "gardening parables" of your own, using your observation of the trees. What spiritual parallels can you draw from the roots and their environment? The exchange of gases, carbon dioxide and oxygen? The creatures that depend on the trees for their life?

In the Bible, God has revealed himself through nature. Which of your observations leap out at you as images of spiritual truths? For example, when you observed the trees, what did you see that illustrates love? Faithfulness? Cooperation? Forgiveness?

One is nearer God's heart in a garden than
anywhere else on earth.
—DOROTHY FRANCES GURNEY

Gardening is an excellent way to observe the cycle of life. You begin by planting the seeds, watering them, watching them grow to maturity and produce fruit (or flowers or vegetables), and eventually seeing them die. But in dying, the plants also produce seeds, which, in turn, spring up with new life.

In the same way, your life also begins with a seed. God helps you grow to maturity so you can produce fruit, in the form of good works and good character. Eventually, we all die. However, as with plants, death is not the end. It merely paves the way to the next phase of life, which is far more wonderful than the first.

A garden is a lovely thing, God has made!
Rose plot,
Fringed pool,
Fern'd grotto—
The surest school
Of peace; and yet the fool
Contends that God is not—
Not God! in gardens! when the eve is cool?
Nay, but I have a sign;
'Tis very sure God walks in mine.

—THOMAS EDWARD BROWN

*They heard the voice of the LORD God walking
in the garden in the cool of the day.*
                                    Genesis 3:8 KJV

A Moment to Refresh

*Awake, north wind, and come, south wind!
Blow on my garden, that its fragrance may
spread abroad.*
                              Song of Solomon 4:16 NIV

*Consider the lilies of the field, how they grow;
they toil not, neither do they spin: and yet I say
unto you, That even Solomon in all his glory
was not arrayed like one of these.*
                                    Matthew 6:28–29 KJV

*My lover has gone down to his garden, to the
beds of spices, to browse in the gardens and to
gather lilies.*
                              Song of Solomon 6:2 NIV

*God said, "Let the land produce vegetation:
seed-bearing plants and trees on the land that
bear fruit with seed in it, according to their
various kinds." And it was so.*
                                    Genesis 1:11 NIV

*To own a bit of ground, to scratch it with a hoe, to plant seeds,
and watch the renewal of life—this is the commonest delight of
the race, the most satisfactory thing a man can do.*

—CHARLES DUDLEY WARNER

*You will be like a garden that has plenty of
water, like a spring of water that never
goes dry.*

Isaiah 58:11 GNT

*Their soul shall be as a watered garden;
and they shall not sorrow any more at all.*

Jeremiah 31:12 KJV

*I am the true vine, and my Father
is the gardener.*

John 15:1 NIV

*God makes grass grow for the cattle, and
plants for man to cultivate.*

Psalm 104:14 NIV

*As the soil makes the sprout come up and a
garden causes seeds to grow, so the
Sovereign LORD will make righteousness
and praise spring up before all nations.*

Isaiah 61:11 NIV

*All that in this
delightful garden
grows, Should
happy be, and have
immortal bliss.*

—EDMUND SPENSER

Expectant Thinking

A Moment to Pause

Pause for a moment and refresh your soul with the hope that God gives—that is that he has a plan for your life and that he will see you through whatever you encounter along the way. Begin by closing your eyes and focusing on one thing you are hoping for—the hope that you will one day graduate, for example. Think about your personal resources that you are hoping will help you reach that goal—your intelligence and diligence and perseverance, perhaps.

You may be placing your hope in many things, like money, fame, education, intelligence. That's great as long as you also realize that those things are all subject to change. There is only one source of hope that will never fail you—that's God. God will see you through—all the way to the final exam, the last paper, the final assignment, and take you on to the next step in his plan for you.

Now focus on another goal you are hoping for—finding a good job when you graduate, for example, or looking for your first apartment. Your hope is well placed in God. The Bible says that those who find their hope in him will never be disappointed.

What oxygen is to the lungs, such is hope for the meaning of life.
EMIL BRUNNER

Hope gives you two pairs of eyes. One pair looks into the past—to see those things that God has done in your life and in the lives of others. This pair will help you to remember that God has always been faithful to you and that he will be faithful in the future as well.

Hope's second pair of eyes looks into the future—to see those things that you are working, dreaming, and praying for. They help you to see and anticipate things like the fulfillment of God's promises and the special plans he has for your life. Open your eyes of hope.

Hope, like the gleaming taper's light,
Adorns and cheers our way;
And still, as darker grows the night,
Emits a brighter ray.

—OLIVER GOLDSMITH

Be strong and take heart, all you who hope in the LORD.

Psalm 31:24 NIV

A Moment to Refresh

You will have confidence, because there is hope; you will be protected and take your rest in safety.

Job 11:18 NRSV

There is hope for a tree that has been cut down; it can come back to life and sprout.

Job 14:7 GNT

Behold, the eye of the LORD *is upon them that fear him, upon them that hope in his mercy.*

Psalm 33:18 KJV

As for me, I will always have hope.

Psalm 71:14 NIV

Show me your ways, O LORD, *teach me your paths; guide me in your truth and teach me, for you are God my Savior, and my hope is in you all day long.*

Psalm 25:4–5 NIV

Hope springs eternal in the human breast; man never is, but always to be blest.

❧

—ALEXANDER POPE

Christ is faithful as a son over God's house. And we are his house, if we hold on to our courage and the hope of which we boast.

Hebrews 3:6 NIV

May the God of hope fill you with all joy and peace as you trust in him, so that you may overflow with hope by the power of the Holy Spirit.

Romans 15:13 NIV

Let us hold fast the confession of our hope without wavering, for He who promised is faithful.

Hebrews 10:23 NASB

I will praise you forever for what you have done; in your name I will hope, for your name is good. I will praise you in the presence of your saints.

Psalm 52:9 NIV

The miserable have no other medicine but only hope.

❧

—WILLIAM SHAKESPEARE

A Slice of Life

A Moment to Pause   Photographs are an excellent way to capture key moments and important milestones in your life such as vacations with your friends and family, holiday and birthday celebrations, and graduation. Other significant moments can occur without a snapshot record.

Think about the significant moments in your life that you haven't captured on film, moments such as the first time you realized God exists, the first time God revealed some important insight to you, or the first time you committed your life to Christ.

Close your eyes and take a mental snapshot of one such moment of spiritual significance, such as the moment you became a Christian. Reflect on that moment in detail beginning with the things like where you were? What you were wearing? Who else was there? Recall what was happening to you on the inside. What was your response to God's love and forgiveness? Once the picture has fully developed, move on to another moment of spiritual significance, such as the first time you shared your faith with someone else.

Keep visualizing these events in your mind until you've assembled a mini photo album of your spiritual life. Think of it as a way to remember all the wonderful things God has done for you.

A good snapshot stops a moment from
running away.
—EUDORA WELTY

A Moment to Reflect

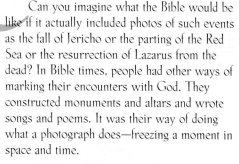

Can you imagine what the Bible would be like if it actually included photos of such events as the fall of Jericho or the parting of the Red Sea or the resurrection of Lazarus from the dead? In Bible times, people had other ways of marking their encounters with God. They constructed monuments and altars and wrote songs and poems. It was their way of doing what a photograph does—freezing a moment in space and time.

God froze the moment when you gave your life to him in space and time by writing your name in his Book of Life.

To see that photo in the album
And that once-familiar face
Brought memories rushing back,
Took me there 'cross time and space.
I thought that I'd forever left
Those people and that place,
But that photo wouldn't let me go
Once I'd been caught in its embrace

—ED STRAUSS

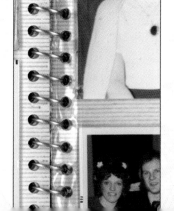

The LORD said to Moses, "Write this on a scroll as something to be remembered."

Exodus 17:14 NIV

A Moment to Refresh

Aaron will bear the names of the sons of Israel over his heart on the breastpiece of decision as a continuing memorial before the LORD.

Exodus 28:29 NIV

These stones shall be to the people of Israel a memorial forever.

Joshua 4:7 NRSV

See the copy of the altar of the LORD which our fathers made, not for burnt offering or for sacrifice; rather it is a witness between us and you.

Joshua 22:28 NASB

I will perpetuate your memory through all generations; therefore the nations will praise you for ever and ever.

Psalm 45:17 NIV

Unlike any other visual image, a photograph is not a rendering, an imitation or an interpretation of its subject, but actually a trace of it. No painting or drawing, however naturalist, belongs to its subject in the way that a photograph does.

—JOHN BERGER

To remember those who do right is a blessing.

Proverbs 10:7 NIRV

What she has done will be told anywhere this good news is preached all over the world. It will be told in memory of her.

Matthew 26:13 NIRV

Those who feared the LORD talked with each other, and the LORD listened and heard. A scroll of remembrance was written in his presence concerning those who feared the LORD and honored his name.

Malachi 3:16 NIV

The camera can photograph thought. It's better than a paragraph of sweet polemic.

—DIRK BOGARDE

Images of the Heart

A Moment to Pause

For a few minutes, plan today to let out the artist inside you. Remember how you might have drawn as a child? Perhaps you portrayed your family as black-crayoned stick figures with round heads, skirts for the females, pants for the boys, all standing under the rays of a smiling sun and in front of a box with a triangle on top—your house.

Get out a piece of paper and some colored pencils. Close your eyes and visualize each of your family members. Short, tall, fat, thin? What shape of face does that person have? Is the hair long, short, or in between? Once you can visualize them clearly, draw what you see.

You almost certainly do not draw the way you did as a child. But your adult drawings can be just as whimsical and appealing if you relax and simply draw a representation of what you see in your mind's eye. Use color to express the special qualities each family member brings to your life—qualities like love, acceptance, wisdom.

When you're finished, write the name of each family member under his or her picture, and as you do, thank God for that person, for his or her unique traits, and for the special things you appreciate about each one.

Other things may change us, but we start and
end with family.
—ANTHONY BRANDT

A Moment to Reflect

When you became a Christian, you also became a member of the largest family in the world: the family of God. That means you have hundreds and thousands of spiritual brothers and sisters that span the centuries.

The family of God doesn't just include those Christians who are alive right now. It includes everyone in every country who ever has followed or who ever will follow Jesus Christ—including some pretty big names from the Bible. When you think of yourself arriving in heaven, picture it as the largest family reunion of all time. Imagine standing beside and linking arms with Mary and Joseph and James and John and all believers.

It's as easy to quarrel with family
As throwing wood upon a fire,
For man is born to trouble,
To lay schemes and to conspire.
But when hardship truly finds you
And your friends all run and hide,
Your family are the only ones
Who'll stand there by your side.

—D. A. CATHCART

117

God setteth the solitary in families.

Psalm 68:6 KJV

A Moment to Refresh

As we have opportunity, let us do good to all people, especially to those who belong to the family of believers.

Galatians 6:10 NIV

Laban said to Jacob, "Surely you are my bone and my flesh."

Genesis 29:14 NASB

Joseph threw his arms around his brother Benjamin and wept, and Benjamin embraced him, weeping. And he kissed all his brothers and wept over them.

Genesis 45:14 NIV

Cornelius and all his family were devout and God-fearing; he gave generously to those in need and prayed to God regularly.

Acts 10:2 NIV

Blood is thicker than water.

—*John Ray*

Honor your father and your mother, as the LORD your God commanded you, so that your days may be long and that it may go well with you in the land that the LORD your God is giving you.
                    Deuteronomy 5:16 NRSV

If any do not take care of their relatives, especially the members of their own family, they have denied the faith and are worse than an unbeliever.
                    1 Timothy 5:8 GNT

Let mutual love continue.
                    Hebrews 13:1 NRSV

Elizabeth's neighbors and relatives heard that the Lord had shown her great mercy, and they shared her joy.
                    Luke 1:58 NIV

The greatest thing in family life is to take a hint when a hint is intended— and not to take a hint when a hint isn't intended.

—*Robert Frost*

Chosen as Beloved

A Moment to Pause

Take a moment, lie back, and relax wherever you feel comfortable. Prepare to escape the bounds of the ordinary and experience God. Imagine this: God—the great God who created the universe, who filled the oceans with water, who set the mountains in place, who created human life—loves you. That truth is so wonderful that it can barely be comprehended and is nearly impossible to fully appreciate. What a glorious day it will be to see him face to face.

Thank God for loving you, for all the times and all the ways he has shown you his love, many of which you may not even have recognized. Ask him to open your heart to experience his love as you never have before.

Think about the tenderness in his hands as he lovingly formed you and planted you in your mother's womb. Think about how he is reaching out to you now, overlooking your faults and drawing you into close relationship with him, all because of his great love. Think about the plans he has carefully prepared for your life, plans more wonderful than you can imagine, all because he loves you so deeply. Now let him know how you feel about him.

The person you are now, the person you have been, the person you will be—this person God has chosen as beloved.
—WILLIAM COUNTRYMAN

A Moment to Reflect

You can earn a degree or a diploma, but you never have to earn God's love—which is certainly a relief, because it is priceless. It is humanly impossible to buy his love, and it is equally impossible to earn it. The only way to have God's love is simply to accept it as his gracious and merciful gift to you.

God's love is an awesome gift that he paid for with the precious blood of his very own son, Jesus Christ. God's love is constant. It never wavers. It was there before you thought of him or knew he existed, and his love will continue for eternity. Live in God's love, and love him in return.

Far from love the Heavenly Father
Leads the chosen child;
Oftener through the realm of briar
Than the meadow mild,
Oftener by the claw of dragon
Than the hand of friend,
Guides the little one predestined
To the native land.

—EMILY DICKINSON

121

Let the beloved of the LORD rest secure in him,
for he shields him all day long.
Deuteronomy 33:12 NIV

A Moment to Refresh

The LORD your God has chosen you out of all
the peoples on the face of the earth to be his
people, his treasured possession.
Deuteronomy 7:6 NIV

Even before the world was made, God had
already chosen us to be his though our union
with Christ.
Ephesians 1:4 GNT

God commendeth his love toward us, in that,
while we were yet sinners, Christ died for us.
Romans 5:8 KJV

I am like an olive tree flourishing in the house
of God; I trust in God's unfailing love for ever
and ever.
Psalm 52:8 NIV

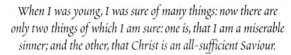

When I was young, I was sure of many things: now there are only two things of which I am sure: one is, that I am a miserable sinner; and the other, that Christ is an all-sufficient Saviour.

—JOHN NEWTON

Brothers and sisters, you are loved by God. We know that he has chosen you.
1 Thessalonians 1:4 NIRV

As those who have been chosen of God, holy and beloved, put on a heart of compassion, kindness, humility, gentleness and patience.
Colossians 3:12 NASB

Beloved, now are we the sons of God, and it doth not yet appear what we shall be: but we know that, when he shall appear, we shall be like him.
1 John 3:2 KJV

May the Lord direct your hearts into God's love and Christ's perseverance.
2 Thessalonians 3:5 NIV

Grace comes into the soul, as the morning sun into the world; first a dawning; then a light; and at last the sun in his full and excellent brightness.

—THOMAS ADAMS

God's Beautiful World

A Moment to Pause

The world God created is infinitely diverse. Take a break just now and go see for yourself. Find a patch of grass and mark off an area about one yard square. Get down on your hands and knees and see how many different forms of life you can find. How many types of grass? How many different bugs or worms or other creepy crawlies? Close your eyes and imagine how many more life forms you could find if you used a microscope.

When you've examined your small square of ground, look up at the trees. What do you see? How many different types of birds, squirrels, leaves, and bark? What scents are in the air? Perhaps you smell the soft fragrance of various flowers, whiffs of honeysuckle lingering on the breeze, or a fresh bouquet of new-mown grass. What sounds catch your ear? Do you hear birds chirping around you, crickets scratching their legs together, or the breeze rustling the leaves overhead?

Stay where you are for several minutes, taking in the sights, sounds, and smells of God's great creation. This small study break can refresh your soul and enable you to hit the books once again with renewed enthusiasm.

Think of the number of trees and blades of grass and flowers, the extravagant wealth of beauty no one ever sees! Think of the sunrises and sunsets we never look at! God is lavish in every degree.

—OSWALD CHAMBERS

A Moment to Reflect

As you contemplate the greatness of God's creation, consider this: The Bible says that you are greater than anything else he has made. Picture the most intriguing creature you can think of, such as a giraffe, a bald eagle, a lion, or a great white shark. These animals may be beautiful, majestic, regal, and powerful, but they've got nothing on you.

That's because, of all the creatures on earth, only you were created in God's own image. Mammals, birds, reptiles, insects, and fish: These are all fantastic creatures, and they all express a different aspect of God's creative activity. But the Bible says that you're the crowning glory of all creation. You're his child.

Nature is what we see,
The Hill, the Afternoon—
Squirrel, Eclipse, the Bumble-bee,
Nay—Nature is Heaven.
Nature is what we know
But have no art to say,
So impotent our wisdom is
To Her simplicity.

—EMILY DICKINSON

125

In the beginning God created the heaven
and the earth.

Genesis 1:1 KJV

A Moment to Refresh

You made the heavens and the stars of the sky.
You made land and sea and everything in them;
you gave life to all.

Nehemiah 9:6 GNT

Who cuts a channel for the torrents of rain, and
a path for the thunderstorm, to water a land
were no man lives, a desert with no one in it?

Job 38:25–26 NIV

The heavens are telling of the glory of God;
And their expanse is declaring the work
of his hands.

Psalm 19:1 NASB

God saw everything that he had made, and
indeed, it was very good.

Genesis 1:31 NRSV

Nature, to be commanded, must be obeyed.

—FRANCIS BACON

How many are your works, O Lord! In wisdom you made them all; the earth is full of your creatures.

Psalm 104:24 NIV

He hath made every thing beautiful in his time.

Ecclesiastes 3:11 KJV

From the very beginning the Word was with God. Through him God made all things; not one thing in all creation was made without him.

John 1:2–3 GNT

From the beginning of creation, God made them male and female.

Mark 10:6 NRSV

Nature, like man, sometimes weeps from gladness.

—BENJAMIN DISRAELI

At Inspirio we love to hear from you—your
stories, your feedback,
and your product ideas.
Please send your comments to us
by way of e-mail at
icares@zondervan.com
or to the address below:

inspirio

Attn: Inspirio Cares
5300 Patterson Avenue SE
Grand Rapids, MI 49530

If you would like further information
about Inspirio and the products we
create please visit us at:
www.inspiriogifts.com

Thank you and God Bless!